BE A NARWHAL

& be cool, be confident, be in control

BE A NARWHAL

& be cool, be confident, be in control

SARAH FORD

ILLUSTRATED BY
ANITA MANGAN

spruce

FOR RACHEL

Narwhal, unicorn of the sea, is a born leader – driven, passionate and full of ideas (mostly good, apart from the time he decided to iron his shirt while wearing it). He leads by example, working hard nine to five to make a living, except on Fridays, when he finishes early to hang out with family and friends. He always gets respect because he leads from the front: 'Everyone follow me!' His office door is always open, though on the odd occasion, when he's let out a small toot, he keeps it shut. He believes in keeping that to himself.

He knows that great things will happen if ideas are shared. His mantra is 'Don't give me problems, give me solutions.' Now if only he could get his coffee machine to work... darned thing's been on the blink for ages.

Narwhal never stops trying and always tackles the worst job first: 'Must reply to that letter from Ronald Rump the walrus about funding his wall.' That done, everything else will be a snorkel in the reef.

There are a few simple things Narwhal knows about living a successful life:

• Paradise is often much closer than you think, like bees on your flowers, shaking your booty to Bob Marley and eating your Granny's stew on a Sunday.

• Comparing yourself to others gets you nowhere. If you've done your best, then that is enough. Though when it comes to plastering, next time Narwhal will fork out for an expert.

• Believe in yourself. You are the bee's knees, even if like Narwhal you don't have any knees.

• Listen more, chatter less – though a morning catch-up on last night's episode of *Love Island* is absolutely essential, over a nice cup of coffee and a ginger snap.

• Think creatively and inspire others with your fabulous ideas: 'Anyone for a seaweed crumpet?'

• Never stop learning. Narwhal thought his Saturday night kebab and Jilly Cooper book ticked that box.

• Success has nothing to do with the size of your bank account. It's all about a life well lived (and still being able to beat your kids at chess).

Narwhal was determined to stop negative thought cycles.

Narwhal was facing
his fears.

Narwhal was keeping
a cool head.

For Narwhal, it was not about black or white.

UP NEXT, THE ARCTIC SYMPHONY ORCA-STRA

Can't be good at everything,
thought Narwhal.

Narwhal wondered
what lesson he could
take from this.

All things must pass,
thought Narwhal.

Narwhal wasn't
afraid to go bold.

Narwhal was not interested in chasing shiny objects.

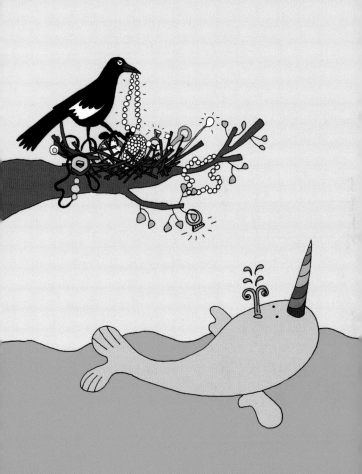

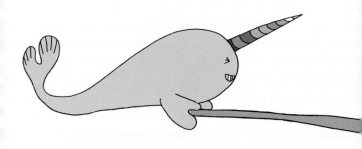

Narwhal was letting go
of what was comforting.

Narwhal had a strong
sense of family.

Narwhal had taken
the higher ground.

Always a silver lining,
thought Narwhal.

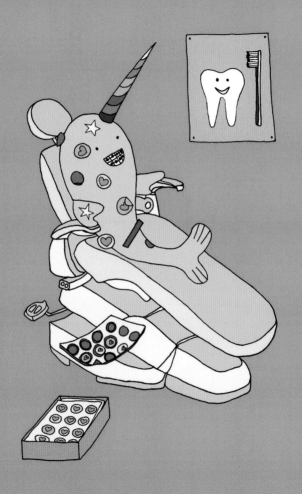

Narwhal thought there was so much to see.

Narwhal decided
not to look back.

Narwhal was in it
for the long run.

Narwhal believed in
equal rights for all.

Narwhal had
taken a risk.

Narwhal always
bounced back.

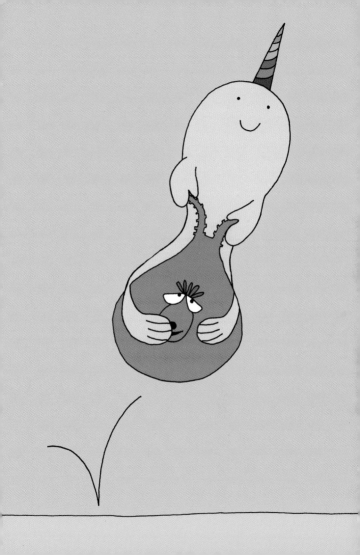

Narwhal liked to try everything once.

Narwhal believed in
telling it like it is.

Narwhal was creating
a bright future.

Narwhal had so
much to say, but
nothing was more
important than
'I love you.'

Narwhal was keeping
his mind and body fit.

Narwhal embraced
new things.

Narwhal was
high on life.

One thing at a time,
thought Narwhal.

Narwhal was exercising restraint.

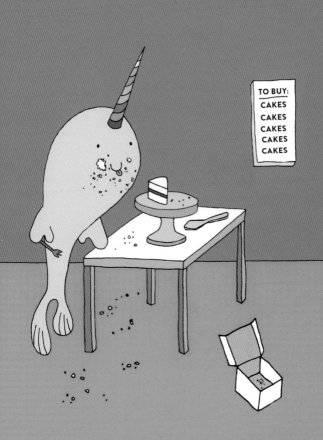

TO BUY:
CAKES
CAKES
CAKES
CAKES
CAKES

Narwhal decided
to just get stuck in.

Today is a new day,
thought Narwhal.

Narwhal knew that everyone
had their own battles.

Narwhal was thinking
fast and slow.

Narwhal had a thirst
for knowledge.

Narwhal wasn't threatened
by brilliant people.

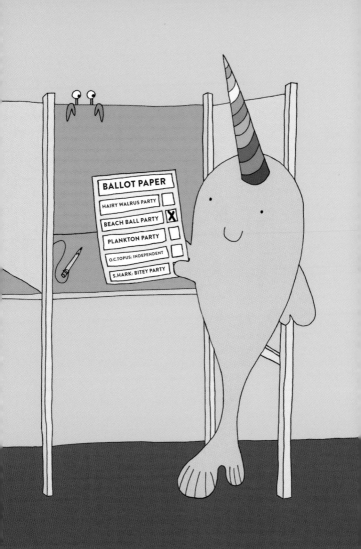

Narwhal always liked
to break the ice.

Narwhal never
stopped trying.

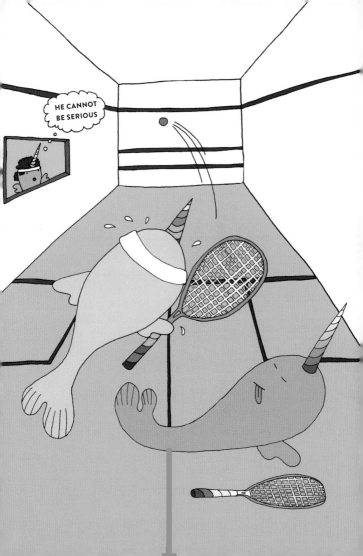

Narwhal always
acknowledged others.

Now be a Narwhal
and make a splash!

An Hachette UK Company
www.hachette.co.uk

First published in Great Britain
in 2019 by Spruce, an imprint of
Octopus Publishing Group Ltd
Carmelite House
50 Victoria Embankment
London EC4Y 0DZ
www.octopusbooks.co.uk

Distributed in the US by
Hachette Book Group
1290 Avenue of the Americas
4th and 5th Floors
New York, NY 10104

Distributed in Canada by
Canadian Manda Group
664 Annette St.
Toronto, Ontario,
Canada M6S 2C8

Sarah Ford asserts the moral right
to be identified as the author of
this work.

ISBN 978-1-84601-585-4

A CIP catalogue record for this
book is available from the British
Library.

Printed and bound in China

10 9 8 7 6 5 4 3 2

Commissioned by
Emily Brickell

Senior Editor
Alex Stetter

Designer and Illustrator
Anita Mangan

Design Assistant
Robyn Shiner

Art Director
Geoff Fennell

Production Controller
Grace O'Byrne